Even Now

Even Now

Poems by

Patricia L. Hamilton

© 2025 Patricia L. Hamilton. All rights reserved.
This material may not be reproduced in any form, published,
reprinted, recorded, performed, broadcast,
rewritten, or redistributed without
the explicit permission of Patricia L. Hamilton.
All such actions are strictly prohibited by law.

Cover design by Shay Culligan
Cover image by Skyler Ewing
Author photo by Lori Ann Cook-Neisler

ISBN: 978-1-63980-695-9
Library of Congress Control Number: 2025932209

Kelsay Books
502 South 1040 East, A-119
American Fork, Utah 84003
Kelsaybooks.com

For the friends I grew up with. You know who you are.

"Like all who write what they remember,
I am inventing the truth."
—Barbara Brown Taylor, *An Altar in the World*

Acknowledgments

The author gratefully acknowledges the original publishers of the following poems, some of which appeared in slightly different versions:

Bindweed: "The Day Everything Changed"
Broad River Review: "Ghost Planes," "Hard Facts," "Idol Worship," "Puzzle," "Trespass"
Common Ground Review: "Heavy Breathing"
Deep South Magazine: "Seizure"
Evening Street Review: "Help Me"
Fare Forward: "Quality of Life"
Homestead Review: "Home Economics," "*Viva la Raza*"
Ibbetson Street: "Condolence," "Fireworks," "Pilgrimage," "Where You Were"
Innisfree Poetry Journal: "Bad Word," "Coming-of-Age Story," "Perfect Afternoon," "The Lesser Evil"
Muddy River Poetry Review: "Missing Out"
Not Very Quiet: "Delinquency"
Our Jackson Home: "Paradise"
Plainsongs: "Crisis," "Lesson Learned," "Lipstick," "The Nature of Inference"
Poem: "Monkey Bars," "Phone Call"
Poetry Porch: "Inventory"
Poetry South: "Aftermath"
Prime Number Magazine: "Counterpoint"
Radical Teacher: "Playbook"
Red River Review: "Even Now," "Gender Roles," "*Passive-Aggressive Handbook* Ch. 17," "The Train from Oxford"
Rushing thru the Dark: "Moonrise," "Random Act of Kindness"
Soul-Lit: "Small Mercies"
Sow's Ear Poetry Review: "With a Y"
Third Wednesday: "Connotation," "Imagination"
Valley Voices: "Paternalism"
The Windhover: "The Moment I Realized," "Twirling"

Contents

One: Even Now

Even Now	15
Missing Out	16
Heavy Breathing	18
With a Y	19
Crisis	20
Where You Were	21
Lesson Learned	22
Monkey Bars	24
Bad Word	25
The Lesser Evil	26
Imagination	27
The Nature of Inference	28
Connotation	29
The Day Everything Changed	31
Free	32
Perfect Afternoon	33
Twirling	35
Phone Call	36
Gender Roles	37
Counterpoint	38
Home Economics	40
Delinquency	42
Moonrise	43
Help Me	45

Two: Before and After

Before and After	49
Coming-of-Age Story	50
Viva la Raza	51

Idol Worship	53
Hard Facts	55
Trespass	57
Passive-Aggressive Handbook Ch. 17: Violence Against Women	59
Small Mercies	61
Paternalism	62
Fireworks	63
Playbook	64
Paradise	66
Random Act of Kindness	68
Seizure	69
Inventory	70
The Train from Oxford	71
The Moment I Realized	72
Aftermath	73
Puzzle	74
Pilgrimage	76
Lipstick	77
Ghost Planes	79
Quality of Life	80
Condolence	82
Notes	85

One: Even Now

Even Now

When I'm out
walking
what unstoppers
the bottle of spiders
I still carry
and sends them
skittering
one by one
down my back:

an ordinary sedan
with tinted windows
idling alone
in a cul-de-sac,
its engine
the deceptive purr
of a cat
biding its time
at a mouse-hole.

Missing Out

I lay in a snarl of sheets,
window open to the twilight
cooling by slow degrees.

Next door, the neighbor's
Rain Bird sprinkler whirred,
tik-tik-tik-tik shhhhhhhhhr.

Quarantined since morning,
I sat up to look out the window.
Nothing to see but the fence.

The scent of wet grass mingled
with the metallic smell
of the screen against my nose.

I flopped back down, dejected,
my siblings long dispatched
to the fairgrounds without me.

I had only a dim notion
of Fourth of July fireworks
but knew I was missing out

on something momentous.
I thrashed, grievance growing.
A gate creaked.

Mr. Ricketts dragged
his trash barrel to the street
as a car swished by.

Shadows swarmed the room,
settling and deepening.
Still I couldn't sleep.

Distant sounds magnified
until I could hear the din
of the fairgrounds crowd,

and a volley of booms
erupted like enemy fire
from a fleet of gunboats,

I a small captive
in the prison ship of my bed,
afloat in the dark, alone.

Heavy Breathing

My mother used to lie on the floor next to my bed
when she feared I would stop breathing,
my exhalations the slow song of a handsaw
laboring to sunder thick hardwood.
At age four, the ministrations of one's mother
never seem extraordinary. I remember only
the scratch tests, grids of sharp pricks across my back
that made me cry. The swift, cooling swabs
of rubbing alcohol that followed
failed to console. I rasped and hiccupped
until the young red-headed nurse
drew me into her lap and rocked me,
her murmurs soothing my sobs
into stuffy-nosed sniffles.

In time I learned a Stoic indifference,
no sigh escaping as I averted my face
from the weekly needles they thought would cure me
but never did. Now morning and evening
I expel a little huff, then draw from my inhaler,
a steady, deep, lung-swelling draft.

With a Y

You can see it in my kindergarten picture:
eyebrows a pair of frustrated logicians,
mouth stretched in a final vowel-squeal
for the patronizing photographer pretending
he can't spell my name. Does he hope I will smile
at his fatuousness? At five, I am already sick
of repeating repeating repeating myself.

y?

What if I yank that glossy tail
right off the horse? What if I drop
that cup and shatter its swooping handle
into shards? What if I snap that twig,
crack! like deadwood?

y not!

i, now. Firecracker ready to *pop! pop!*
Exclamation point standing on its head.
Morse code *n* enjoying a snooze.
Delicate neck of a yellow-eyed daisy.
i is dainty, raising her pinkie as she sips.
Knees together, ankles crossed.
No fidgeting. No giggling.

No fun.

Oh, *y!* Let me shimmy up your rope
to Tarzan-swing in dashing figure-eights.
Let me clamber into your saddle for a gallop,
then plummet down your slide headfirst. And
when I'm tuckered out, I'll snuggle into your crook.

i? Bye-bye!

Crisis

The crisis is never what you think.
When Mrs. Foster heard me crying
in the line outside our kindergarten classroom
she didn't expect her hand to come away bloody
from a gesture meant to soothe.
For Mary Rose, standing right behind me,
the issue was credibility: would she be believed
if she swore she was not the instigator
of the push that cracked the back of my head
on the edge of the propped-open, metal door?
For my mother, logistics became the challenge
once she got the call from the school secretary
that every mother dreads: should she drive me
to Dr. Long's or straight to the ER to get stitches?

Since every five-year-old girl knows
unruly boys in the back of the line
keen to demonstrate their prowess
are the proximate cause of the regular swells
that jostle small bodies against each other,
Mary Rose, needlessly distressed,
was exonerated of any wrong-doing in my eyes.
Mrs. Foster, who mimed patting my head,
then seeing blood, was cleared in my mother's.
Dr. Long calmly sutured the gash.
The real crisis—the one still echoing
across the decades—was how many years,
how many knocks on the head it took me to realize
I could move to the back of the line.

Where You Were

Friday, 10:30 a.m. PST, when gunshots
stilled the earth's spin: At school
carefully printing alphabet letters
between the paper's dotted blue lines,
sounding out words about Puff and Spot.
After lunch the teachers, looking grave,
agreed "assassination" was a word
above your comprehension level.

Friday, 2:30 p.m. PST, Air Force One *en route*
to Washington: On Bus Number 5, KFXM blaring,
Lesley Gore wailing that you'd cry, too,
if it happened to you. At your stop you charged off,
heedless of Don the Bus Driver's sad head-shake,
barreling with your playmates into their house.
Their mother and sister, glued to the TV,
shushed the three of you: "The President's been shot."

Saturday, 8:00 a.m. PST: In your room, aggrieved
that Saturday morning cartoons weren't on,
even the ones you didn't normally watch.
You emerged to check the TV again just in case,
but every channel featured men talking, talking,
talking in somber tones. Your parents were silent,
grim-faced. You did not understand, even after
your brother and sister said, "no school on Monday."

Monday, 8:30 a.m. PST: On the living room couch,
your only previous experience of death a phone call
that made your mother cry. On TV a mass of people
marched solemnly behind a flag-draped coffin
led by a black-veiled woman. Earlier you glimpsed her
holding the hands of two children. Your mother tried
to explain, but you were still uncertain, confused.
As you learned much later, so was the rest of the country.

Lesson Learned

Naturally, I burst into tears.
No one had ever told me
one day I might tumble off the school bus,
wave goodbye to TJ,
and fling open my front door
to find no one home.
I stood clutching my Flintstones lunchbox.
Where was my mother?

Into the house's long, perfidious silence
a knock thundered.
No one had ever told me
not to answer the door when I was alone,
so I opened it.

Trumpet case in hand, Brian Shumway
stood on the front step, ready to practice
a beginner's version of "The Carnival of Venice"
with my sister at the piano.
"Nobody's here!" I blurted.
He gaped at my tear-streaked face,
then shuffled back to his mother's station wagon
purring at the curb.

That evening my mother reproached me
for crying. I was a big girl now.
I needed to show some resourcefulness
next time I found myself alone.

A few weeks later a Chrysler glided up
beside the patch of dirt where TJ and I
were digging a parking garage
 for our tiny plastic cars.
Lucille, my father's kind-faced secretary,
leaned toward the open passenger window
and said she'd been sent to fetch me.
My mother had been detained.
Placidly I replied I would be fine where I was
and kept digging. Astonished,
Lucille tried to coax me to come with her
but eventually drove back to the bank
without me.

Everyone had forgotten
what they'd always told me:
Never
accept any ride
you haven't asked for.

Monkey Bars

My aspiration was to travel far.
I learned my limitations all too soon.
I could not swing across the monkey bars.

I mastered reading like I was a czar.
I treasured each day's lesson like a rune.
My aspiration was to travel far.

The playground proved a training ground for war.
The rigor was enough to make me swoon.
I could not swing across the monkey bars.

Boys dreamed of riding rocket ships to Mars.
Girls seldom dared to think they'd reach the moon.
My aspiration was to travel far.

I tried my hardest. All I got was scars.
Some days I ate my lunch alone at noon.
I could not swing across the monkey bars.

Our teachers told us we could reach the stars,
but that dream shriveled like a popped balloon.
My aspiration was to travel far.
I could not even swing across the bars.

Bad Word

Red spots flaring on her copper cheeks,
raven-haired Rosa spat a single word
into the playground dirt,
raising a small puff of dust.
It sounded like an arrow whooshing past
to stick in a rough-barked tree trunk.
After recess some pint-sized prosecutor
charged Rosa before our frowning teacher
and called me as a witness.
Did I or did I not hear her say a bad word?
I hardly knew. I tried to conjure its sound:
a sigh with a fishhook on the end.
Which part was bad?
I weighed my choices: snitch or shrug?
Rosa remained mute, smoke-black eyes
giving nothing away.

Years later I recognized the word,
realized she was guilty. Did her escape
from the fierce tether-ball slap
of schoolyard justice tame her tongue?
Or did she take up target practice,
arrow-straight epithets hitting every mark,
final consonants pinning their victims
with the precision of a knife-thrower?

The Lesser Evil

I would describe
my throat as
a raging fire
to Mrs. Palmer,
the school secretary,
so I wouldn't
have to wait
for my mother
after school, standing
on the corner
across from where
the man tending
the church's lawn
watched, sitting in
his old Pontiac
in the shade,
ready to kidnap
girls like me
and do things
I could not,
at seven, imagine
or name, yet
feared.

Imagination

Every day I pored over the Christmas catalog,
my annual ritual, memorizing each doll I coveted,
each board game I required, each sleek bicycle
with rainbow streamers summoning me
to the open road. I was captivated
by the party dresses with stiff, lacy skirts
I thought Shirley Temple would be proud to wear.

Then one night: magic.
After my mother turned out my bedroom light,
I snuggled under the covers, trying to picture
the dresses I admired. Inexplicably
my mind began fashioning new ones—
out of air, out of nothing!—
red velvet paired with rich plaid,
white satin whirled with snowflake blue,
deep emerald trimmed with shiny gold ribbon.
The next night, I squeezed my eyes shut, fearful
the colors and patterns would no longer kaleidoscope
through my mind. But conjuring them
required only a tiny "what if?"
As my new power dazzled me off to dreamland,
I wondered why no one had ever hinted at such a gift,
better than any other I could wish for.

The Nature of Inference

When she was angry
our second-grade teacher
threatened to tear us
"limb from limb"—her
exact words, chin defiant.
"I can, you know."

Reasoning from her strong,
broad hands, her enormous
girth, and the fierce
light in her eyes,
we believed her. Every
last one of us.

Connotation

Growing up sheltered, I scarcely ever heard a racial slur.
The *n*-word, perhaps, on my kindergarten playground—
I hurled it at my sister once and promptly
got a spanking. Later interrogation revealed
I had no clue what it meant, despite glimpses
of riots erupting on our black-and-white TV
before my mother or father could snap it off.
Some words in print like *Jap* I puzzled out:
the Nishinos, who ran our town's florist and nursery
and who'd suffered in some mysterious, unnamed
way during the war, before I was born, were Japanese.
Others like *Chink*—the eye-shaped hole in our weathered
back fence, under which my brother's beagle
was forever digging his way out—baffled. And *Dago?*
Spanish for "dog," maybe? The dictionary was no help.

So years later I felt abashed when a friend
scolded me for saying *wetback*
instead of "undocumented worker."
Throughout my childhood whenever we saw
brown-skinned men in their floppy hats
stooped over, picking strawberries,
or high up on ladders, harvesting oranges,
my mother twisted her lips in sympathy,
remembering how her arms had ached from reaching
to pluck ripe apricots every summer, sweat trickling
down her forehead into her eyes. Her father
had followed the seasonal crops from San Diego
to Walla Walla, moving from one labor camp
to the next, the whole family in tow, grateful
for any work at all. "Itinerant," she called him.

I must've asked her once what *wetback* meant,
not yet understanding metaphor, unable
to tease out the meaning for myself. She told me
people swam across the river to find work
when they were hungry enough. What river?
I wondered. All I'd ever seen were dry beds,
desiccated mudflats, spills of granite and silt.
My finger found an answer in our atlas,
a thin blue line I traced across vast tracts
of wilderness that conjured up images I'd seen
in *National Geographic* of narrow river canyons
widening into shallow currents. Who could imagine
that word to be an insult? I pictured only strong men,
providers, stroking steadily toward the dignity of labor,
their glossy black heads backlit by a golden sun.

The Day Everything Changed

The English Professor Reminisces

In
the fifth
grade I longed
to become a writer.

But
now I
see my fate
was sealed the day

Mr. Cheney was called
away from class.
He handed
me

our reading group's text
and told me
to carry
on.

Free

In those days kids were free to roll around
in the back of a station wagon, unharnessed,
which was how Mary and I coped with all the curves
and switchbacks through the chaparral and live oak
as her family's Chevrolet snaked along Ortega Highway,
her father piloting us with a firm hand
up over the Santa Ana range and down to Doheny Beach,
Carol and her friend Cindy chattering in the backseat.
To appease my stomach's queasiness,
once we'd parked, Mary's mother offered me a cream soda:
a new flavor to celebrate a new beach, I untethered
from my family for the first time.
The ocean sparkled under the hazy sun.
While the adults set up blankets and umbrellas,
the older girls sauntered off in search of boys to ogle,
disregarding parental cautions. Mary and I trailed behind,
watching the seagulls soar and swoop, unbound
by time or expectation. After a lazy picnic lunch,
we four linked arms and jumped the waves
as they curled and broke. Our knees washed in foam,
the spume smelling of fish and seaweed,
we belted out "I wanna be free-e-e" to the sea and sky
as if the Monkees' chart-climbing ballad were an anthem,
not a song about safe distances, about rule-setting by men.
Exhilaration pulsed through our limbs
as we leapt and splashed unfettered,
the adults waving benignly from their encampment,
the marine layer only a thin grey line on the horizon,
our hearts open, unravaged.

Perfect Afternoon

My bedroom windows open to a breeze
stirring the curtains, I sprawled on the floor,
sixth-grade science text pushed aside,

listening to the Mamas and the Papas proclaim
undying dedication to the ones they loved
in harmonies lush as the sweet spring air,

the record-player needle emitting a staticky pop
every time it hit a scratch on the vinyl.
From the kitchen came the sizzle of hot Crisco

as the aroma of frying chicken, crisp and golden,
filled the house, the rhythmic *thwack*
of my mother's knife promising potato salad.

The previous year, the evening news had gut-punched us
night after night with the unthinkable—
crumpled bodies felled by soldiers or assassins.

But I'd learned the television screen was like a window:
I could gaze at the view or look away,
taking comfort in the artifacts of family life around me.

Now, as a blue jay squawked outside
in the tender-leafed mulberry tree, white alyssum
wafting its honey through the windows,

the world's din seemed remote. I was contented,
tapping my foot to the exuberant music's percussive beat,
unaware that all too soon

ringing phones would shatter our deep sleep,
and I would start learning sorrow's slow, aching melody,
my heart pounding in the dark each time

I strained to decipher my father's murmur,
my mother's reply, wondering whose death
had ripped an unmendable hole in the universe.

Twirling

The church foyer was empty
except for Pam and me.
We twirled in place
to make our skirts swish
and flare out like an ice-skater's
floating on air. Joy, fizzing up
as if shaken in a soda bottle,
spurred us to spin ourselves dizzy.

"Girls!" a woman's voice reprimanded,
"this is the house of God!"
Mrs. G. stood glaring at us, her hair
perfectly coiffed, her patent stilettos gleaming.
The word "God" echoed
as if the steel door of a vault
had slammed shut
at the end of a marble corridor.

Chastened, we desisted.
But for years I've wondered
at the vast chasm between Mrs. G's god—
cold and dour, as if carved in stone—
and ours: ebullient Maker of tiny whorled shells,
of whirling, white-ruffled eddies,
of glittering galaxies spiraling their way
across the vast black night sky.

Phone Call

"What's artillery?" I pleaded the night my brother
phoned from Fort Ord, the color draining
from my parents' faces my only answer.

I'd seen hippies waving peace-sign placards
at army trucks lumbering along the highway
like a line of elephants, trunk to tail,

but, preoccupied with wardrobing my Barbie,
didn't fathom the mechanics of war.
Flash forward to another fragmentary memory:

dense clouds hovering over Newport Beach,
the surprising destination to which my father
had driven us, a deviation from Sunday routine,

my brother in his dress uniform, shoes shiny.
We strolled, we ate at a restaurant, a treat
to make his last hours memorable, everything

swathed in the mute gray mist of things left unsaid.
Despite the airport's cheerful bustle and swirl,
a rockslide cascaded into my stomach

during our somber march to the gate,
the blue-and-green-tiled tunnel endless,
sadness magnified by every footfall.

My parents—always so diffident,
already fearing the next phone call—
how did they say goodbye?

All I remember, before our sad drag
back through the tunnel, is the fog
pressing against the plate glass windows.

Gender Roles

My mother always bought wedding gifts at the hardware store,
a corner redbrick fronted by a line of date palms
in the first block of downtown, facing McPherson's Furniture
and my father's bank. Gibbel's to everyone,
even after the owner died and the family sold.
Kitchenware on the right as you walked in—
mixers, pots and pans—and along the back wall, fine china.
Five-piece place settings—flawless white and ivory
with gold or silver rims and floral borders, densely intricate
or delicately sprigged in the palest pastels—
each pattern elegant, unlike the plain melamine we ate on at home.
The bridal registry—white leather embossed with silver letters—
bore the names of each engaged couple with their choices
for china, silver, and crystal carefully written out,
an index of domestic desire, teaching me to hope
one day I'd be empress of my own table
with brocade napkins and impossibly thin-stemmed goblets.

Offerings on the left side of the store were more prosaic—
scissors, flashlights, canning jars, electric fans—
all bathed in the bright light pouring through the front windows,
where displays of canister sets and exotic teak salad bowls
beckoned housewives inside to browse. I never
crossed the boundary into the store's cavern-like back,
at least not on my own. If my father needed a drill bit
or some caulk, he always used the rear entrance.
Whenever I tagged along, I stuck close to his side
in that dark den of saw blades and rasps,
rakes and spades hanging on a pegboard wall,
camping lanterns dangling from rafters,
the aisles between towering shelves lit by naked bulbs.
The way the grizzled men behind the counter
who spoke the gruff language of painters and plumbers
cut their eyes toward me as I hovered at my father's elbow
confirmed I was trespassing where a girl could never belong.

Counterpoint

Mr. Stoa taught us Bartók, notes clustered in discordant patterns
like words with too many consonants.
One Saturday when we rehearsed at his apartment
he disappeared into the bedroom to tend to his wife's needs.

Like words with too many consonants
her disease, scleroderma, was hard to pronounce.
He disappeared into the bedroom to tend to his wife's needs,
hoping she'd be cheered by our junior-high exuberance.

Her disease, scleroderma, was hard to pronounce.
We were young, inexperienced with mortality,
hoping she'd be cheered by our junior-high exuberance.
"That monkey!" a father sniped behind Mr. Stoa's back.

We were young, inexperienced with mortality,
with prejudice against the unfamiliar.
"That monkey!" a father sniped behind Mr. Stoa's back,
frowning at our teacher's beard and Birkenstocks.

With prejudice against the unfamiliar,
our parents kept a watchful eye on us,
frowning at our teacher's beard and Birkenstocks.
How Mr. Stoa loved Bach—motets, partitas, fugues.

Our parents kept a watchful eye on us
although Top Hits radio taught us all about Woodstock.
How Mr. Stoa loved Bach—motets, partitas, fugues—
weaving Baroque music into our lives as a labor of love.

Although Top Hits radio taught us all about Woodstock,
we practiced stately sarabandes on our recorders,
weaving Baroque music into our lives as a labor of love
at that gangly age when interests careen in all directions.

We practiced stately sarabandes on our recorders
while the nightly news focused on draft dodgers and riots.
At that gangly age when interests careen in all directions,
we held a pancake breakfast to raise money for a harpsichord.

While the nightly news focused on draft dodgers and riots,
the wife's fingers grew slack from the effort to hold on.
We held a pancake breakfast to raise money for a harpsichord,
only dimly guessing at the heartbreak that lay ahead.

The wife's fingers grew slack from the effort to hold on.
One Saturday when we rehearsed at his apartment,
only dimly guessing at the heartbreak that lay ahead,
Mr. Stoa taught us Bartók, notes clustered in discordant patterns.

Home Economics

That week with my sister in Modesto, the kitchen radio
played an endless loop of The Doors' "Riders on the Storm"—
Jim Morrison's deadpan chant the anchor for moody riffs
on the Fender Rhodes, haunted by rain and claps of thunder—
alternating with Carole King crooning it was too late,
both songs pulsing along the same hypnotic 4/4 groove
in a minor key suited to the duplex's dimness, the shades
pulled to block the fiery afternoon sun. While the baby napped,
I read, savoring the breeze stirred up by an oscillating fan.
I could hear my sister muttering curses at the weevils
she'd found in her flour, her second year of marriage
marked by cloth diapers and other domestic economies.
Like a cryptic prophet, Jim warned of a sinister killer lurking
in plain sight, Carole's prognostication of imminent break-up
feeling just as remote. When the news came on at five,
I headed to the kitchen to peel potatoes, an eager helper.
My mother thought cooking from scratch an absurdity,
but my sister relished creation and innovation. That week
I practiced rolling out pie crusts and beating egg whites.
Twice we treated ourselves to French toast for breakfast.

That week, too, I made a dress under my sister's tutelage.
I'd been dogging her through fabric stores for years.
Eighth-grade sewing had been wasted on useless drawstring bags,
but now I was learning how to match plaids and clip curves
before ironing them flat. When my brother-in-law returned
from his long shift running peaches at the cannery, I fed the baby
his strained carrots while my sister put a meatloaf on the table,
the radio lower now but Jim—dead in Paris of a heroin overdose—
still intoning that a girl should love her man. Carole sadly replied
that she could no longer fake it. Once we'd dried and put away
the dishes, we sat on the front stoop as the sprinkler doused
the red hibiscus. When my brother-in-law retired to bed,
his alarm set for four a.m., my sister gave the baby his bath,
I at her elbow observing the rituals of powdering. At fourteen
and twenty-three, listening to that soundtrack, what did we know
of nihilism parading about in the tatters of flagrant excess?
Or slow-simmering heartache scorching love and boiling it dry?
We knew only what we'd been told mattered:
gratitude for shelter, appreciation for nourishing food,
thankfulness for well-constructed clothing that would last.

Delinquency

Student Conference Day:
classes cancelled. Freshmen,
we were rabbits with quivering noses
sprung free from our cages.

*We were the smart girls. Straight
A's. Evenings filled with algebra.
Always first to raise our hands.*

By afternoon, upperclassmen fleeing,
no narcs to patrol the parking lots.
We kicked off our shoes and plopped
onto the lawn in front of the office.

*We were the shy girls. Invisible
in hallways. Untutored in flirting.
Doomed to miss all proms.*

"Hi, girls!" The principal, smiling,
oblivious to our casually crossed hands,
to the odd pile in our midst
(two erasers, a stick of gum, a comb).

*We were the good girls. Never
whispering in the back row. Never
passing notes or ditching class.*

"Hi, girls!" The vice-principal, waving.
But our band director, usually unflappable,
back-tracked, loomed over us, frowned.
"You girls playing *poker?*"

Moonrise

"Tropical" summoned picture-book toucans,
"sultry" a word I'd only read.
But this air was alive—leaf-riffling eddies,
frond-flashing currents swirling
through bougainvillea-bright pinks and reds,
the warm sea-scent sweeping our taxi
through a vibrant cityscape stitched with tourist-trade
to our hotel, sentried by purple-orange Birds of Paradise,
afternoon clouds mounding in white masses on the horizon.

I'd encountered aquamarine—
my birthstone, the pool I swam in each summer.
But this water astonished, an exuberance of blues,
pale shallows striated into pellucid azure,
wisp-shadows dappling the sparkling sheen,
beach-bathers beading the white sand-necklace
as transistors blared over children's squeals,
in the distance the rumpled brown pleat-folds
of Diamond Head ascending to their iconic peak.

Dixieland was familiar
from summer band concerts in the park.
But this jazz burned a hole in the night,
the combo in the courtyard bar conversing
at a lazy island tempo, smart-alecky trumpet
trading barbs with a growling trombone,
both sweet-talking the clarinet, whose sassy replies
were sinuous as the breeze, the sound of surf breaking
on the beach as steady as the drummer's brushwork.

I'd gazed at the moon
hanging above the mountains that flanked my hometown.
But this moon seared itself into my memory:
a perfect, luminous orb ascending serenely
behind silhouetted coconut palms and glittering hotels,
the fresh ocean air ruffling my hair as I sat on the balcony,
reluctantly left behind by aunties off to see Don Ho,
reveling in my solitude, entranced by the night-music—
a gift as exotic and intoxicating as a sip from a magic potion.

Help Me

A vivid memory, no reason: Spring sunshine,
lazing on the lawn behind the band room after lunch,
bees bobbling in the clover, Joni Mitchell crooning "Help Me."

Days drowning in duty: High-school French,
chemistry homework, Bach partitas on the piano,
clarinet lessons every Friday, no thought of crying "Help me!"

Joni's voice a starry sky: Deep midnight
spiraled with light, her highest notes sparkling
diamonds to make you forget she's pleading "Help me."

The heavens a hopeful blue: A cloudless canvas
awaiting a skywriter who'll dip and swoop overhead
to tell me who I might become, never once scrawling "Help me."

Joni's lyrics a revelation: A curtain parted
on a couple swaying to a lazy riff in smoky light,
the woman, knowing all the signs, murmuring "Help me."

My future unfathomed: To break free, how much
must I unlearn, unknow, undo? And will anyone answer
when I look up to that same mute sky and whisper "Help me"?

Two: Before and After

Before and After

A few moments
hold up a flaming torch
to kindle the understanding;
the rarest ones set the memory on fire.

But as the gnomon's edge on a sundial
delineates light from shadow,
so every moment divides
before from after.

Coming-of-Age Story

After college we transformed ourselves with contact lenses
and acrylic nails, acquiring credit cards and new-car loans,
growing toward womanhood like vines
twining their tendrils toward the sunlight.
At the year mark we felt mild surprise
when the classmate with the fusty name—
a timorous soul, trapped behind tortoise-shell glasses,
her homemade clothes never in style,
her only vividness a helmet of flame-red hair—
was the first among us to get married.

One Thursday eight months later her newlywed husband
dropped by after work on a gleaming Harley Super Glide
to see our new roommate, a honey-tongued blonde
who'd answered the ad we'd placed to cope with our steep rent—
an old friend from way back, he explained
as she hopped on the bike behind him and clamped her hands
on his slender hips to take a spin around the block.
He's merely showing off his new toy, we thought. Men did that.
But the next Thursday the ride was longer, and reportedly faster,
wind whipping their hair as they careened through the hills.

And so it went. Our roommate denied it meant anything,
insisting a little harmless indulgence never hurt anyone.
But when she unwrapped her arms from his waist
and slung her leg off the bike, she always lingered
at the curb, the two talking long into the dinner hour.
Hearing the engine's slow throb, we would creep
into the living room and peer through the half-open blinds,
helpless as a Greek chorus, unable to avert our eyes
as if we were watching a scene from a forbidden film,
one whose ending we knew we were not going to like.

Viva la Raza

Saturdays I would wake to tuba-heavy Mexican polka music
thumping from someone's car radio across the street. Too early,

but it was a free country, and my duplex—Spanish-style stucco
with a flat, red-tiled roof—was on the fringe of a *barrio,*

not gang-ridden like you'd hear about on the news, just shabby,
with wrought-iron window bars and graffiti-sprayed cinder block.

Commonwealth Avenue, a name in which I saw no irony,
was a busy, four-lane buffer for all but sound waves. On my side

the haves were barely hanging on, mostly college students,
single moms, a few retirees, the tiny lots crammed with cottages,

vibrant hibiscus and blowsy roses in even the smallest yards.
I would indulge in $1.99 pancakes and coffee at Zono's

to gear up for my weekly ordeal at the laundromat. I didn't mind
the steamy heat, the cloying smells of bleach and fabric softener,

as much as the bold stares of the *cholos* whose eyes slid down
my bare arms to my breasts and lingered. Laborers, they slouched

in white undershirts with wide armholes that revealed their ribs
as their work clothes released the week's grime into sudsy water.

Nose in a book, I'd avoid their smoldering gazes, pretending
a dotted line no one could cross encircled me. No one

followed me home. But later, when I'd take my bicycle for a spin,
the catcalls always came from an ancient pickup truck, bulging

with young Hispanic men, slowing as it passed. A woman
in public, I was subject to comment, or ululation. Eyes focused

on the bike lane, I kept pedaling toward the railroad bridge
emblazoned with *"Viva la Raza."* It never occurred to me

cholos didn't have the right to share the street, or the laundromat.
There were washing machines enough, and roadway, for all.

Idol Worship

Chengdu, 1985

When the Class President announced
our Saturday field trip's destination—
the Hall of Five Hundred Buddhas—
my stomach sank. But I knew my cue
as a foreign teacher: smile at the chance
to honor my students' cultural heritage.

That's all it was to them. Mao was dead,
but the Party continued to ban belief
in any Ultimate Cause but itself.
All around whispered tales still whirled
of exiled uncles cracking rocks
with pick-axes in the countryside.

We bumped at breakneck speed
over the mud-rutted roads to Xindu,
my fourteen English-teacher charges
and I crammed into a small white van.
Silently I prayed for safety as we jostled
against each other, kidney-jarred.

We lunched on boiled *jiaozi* and warm beer
in a sweltering hovel, then split up.
The Buddha hall was cool and quiet, a relief.
Alone, I walked the long aisles,
each lined with painted terra cotta figures,
every pose, every gesture, distinctive.

With each statue I studied, my admiration
grew for the ancient artisans who could depict
such an array of silken robes in exquisite hues,
each somber brow or benign smile unique.
Guard lowered, I never sensed
the crouching tiger that lay ahead.

In the hall's center, the Boddhisatva Guanyin—
her dozen hands outstretched—
towered over a ring of kneeling worshippers
bowing low with burning sticks of incense.
Here was a brazen show of veneration,
surely risky, given Party prohibitions.

In my own religious tradition, idol worship
was anathema. My mind flailed for balance,
teetering between repulsion and respect.
Seeing my confusion, my student Mrs. Du,
a decade my senior, stepped forward.
"Do you believe in God?" she demanded.

I would never deny my faith by saying "no."
But before I could explain, "Not one made
by human hands," Mrs. Du turned away
with a dismissive smirk, consigning me
to the company of the idolatrous, her question
a kung fu master's kick to my unprotected gut.

Hard Facts

The first: so ordinary.
She has to leave class early on Friday.

I hear it all the time.
But not for that reason.

The sucker punch:
Her mother is driving her.

*

Alone, later: deep breaths.
She doesn't want my advice.

Then why even tell me?
Schemes tumble through my mind.

I count costs, make projections.
I barely make enough to get by.

*

Irony: the weekend is sunny.
She has her whole life before her.

So her mother says.
"She only wants what's best."

I cradle my mourning close.
So do we all.

*

Monday: calm surfaces.
Every action has an equal and opposite.

Two absences follow.
When she returns, her eyes are dead.

What is my role?
I am involved in humankind.

*

New grief: sharp as sorrow's longing.
There was a second one.

This one glimpsed onscreen.
She exits the empty classroom, eyes brimming.

The breath sucks out of me.
I will never feel more childless.

Trespass

Now I see it was a set-up, that mild December day
we parked my boyfriend's battered Civic in the hard-packed
dirt lot and followed the runnel-gouged road
on foot until it petered into a narrow, rutted trail
that wound through chaparral-covered flanks and folds
shaded by scrub oak and Manzanita,
then climbed and dipped and rose, cresting
on a grassy ridge open to the scudding clouds.
JD came with us since the two of them
had crossed the Karakoram together into China,
their version of a buddy-movie storyline.
I was resigned to my role as the girl—winded too soon,
needing to pause for a swig of water, lagging
on the steepest slopes—but trying hard to be plucky,
never realizing a threesome always meant
two would outvote one. Once we reached
the blustery summit, newly green after a soaking rain,
I stood slightly apart, drinking in the sage-scented air,
surveying the cottonwood-clotted valley far below
where we'd arranged for my best friend to retrieve us.

When he lifted the barbed-wire, I didn't sense my doom,
didn't realize whatever I chose would mean failing his test.
Baffled at the Sunday School moralist turned maverick,
the rule-follower ignoring the posted warning, perhaps
I should have recognized there had been other tests,
some quite cunning. But cruelty was a foreign tongue
I could never decipher. When JD thrust his leg
through the spread wires as if capitulation
were a long habit, I was too dumbstruck to do anything
but bend to the blithe force of my boyfriend's will.
Soon the security guard of the munitions plant
on whose land we were trespassing

blazed uphill in his pickup to bawl us out,
tumbleweed-cloud of dust rolling behind.
On the bronco-ride down to the guard shack
JD joked about *The Dukes of Hazzard.*
The boyfriend kept his own counsel. I held on tight
to the truck bed's side, quivering like a rabbit
in a sprung trap. The hacked-off guard jolted to a stop,
hollered again about idiot hikers, then let us go.

That night at the church party, I wanted to savor
the Christmas carols, the candles, the hot cocoa,
grateful for the guard's grace despite our foolishness.
We were safe, I thought, chastened but unscathed.
I was ready to forgive, move on. But the boyfriend
wouldn't look at me, wouldn't speak, wouldn't tell me
what was wrong. Some unspoken boundary breached?
For years I tormented myself with his silence,
unable to grasp the one sin he couldn't forgive:
my not hating him as much as he hated himself.

Passive-Aggressive Handbook Ch. 17:
Violence Against Women

Choose someone compliant,
soft as a mattress that retains
your imprint after you rise.

An only child, unschooled
in spilling secrets or sparring,
unused to the quick deflective jab,

unpracticed with men.
All the better if she's eager to please,
a sunflower leaning, yearning.

Smile often, but never make promises.
Keep your lines untangled
and your bait fresh.

Increase her trust, steadily
twisting the knob on the stove
until the flame burns bright blue.

Let her meet the family
as if making steady progress
up a steep, rocky trail.

When spring warmth stirs,
suggest watching the moonrise.
Drive somewhere remote.

She will expect romance.
Spring the trap:
"What would you do if . . . ?"

Enjoy watching her confusion
turn to terror
as she realizes her utter isolation.

But make sure
you lock up
every scrap of paper in the world.

Pitch the key into the black night.
If ever she finds a pen,
she'll write a scream to last forever.

Small Mercies

An exercise
to strengthen the heart:
she writes down the names
of family members
and begins to pray,
desiring to forgive
past wrongs.

Third on the list:
her grandfather, dead
before she was three.
Inexplicably
sobs erupt,
wrenching, wracking,
tectonic plates colliding.

Her only memory:
a blurred figure,
she crying,
squirming in arms
to keep him at bay.
All else blank, no matter
how hard she tries.

Paternalism

I learned the meaning of paternalism—
its aim to encase women in starched white aprons—
over punch at my parents' fiftieth anniversary party:
A stranger asked me if I'd ever thought of marrying.

Its aim to encase women in starched white aprons,
the question hit me like a whack with a plank.
A stranger asked me if I'd ever thought of marrying
as if a woman of thirty-one in low heels posed a threat.

The question hit me like a whack with a plank,
coming from a married colleague of my father,
as if a woman of thirty-one in low heels posed a threat—
as if the matter were the business of a perfect stranger.

Coming from a married colleague of my father,
disguised by a smile of friendly interest
as if the matter were the business of a perfect stranger,
the man's presumption stunned me.

Disguised by a smile of friendly interest
over punch at my parents' fiftieth anniversary party,
the man's presumption stunned me.
I learned the meaning of paternalism.

Fireworks

Born too late, I missed all those Gidget surfer movies,
watching only the Sally Field TV version in reruns.
I remember nothing but Moondoggie's name
and the furrowed brow of the widowed father
as he tried to corral his boy-crazy teen.
By the time a sequel, *Gidget Grows Up,*
aired on *Movie of the Week,* I was on the verge
of puberty, not quite interested in specific boys
but absorbing various tropes of television romance.
During Gidget's glamorous stint as a UN tour guide,
she fell for an older man. But then Moondoggie/Jeff
showed up in his crisp Air Force uniform and proposed
as brilliant Fourth of July fireworks filled the sky,
breathtaking night-blooms reflecting in the East River.

I never told anyone the ideal I developed from that movie.
Such notions imprint on us without our knowing.
Imagine my shock years later when my grad school boyfriend
drove me to our local mall on July 3 to watch fireworks,
our heads craned upward as we stood surrounded
by parked cars. Enthralled by squealing rockets
and glittery showers of light, my boyfriend—
now my husband—suddenly scrambled
to rummage in the car's glove compartment,
fumbled with a small box, and dropped to one knee,
the national anthem's blaring through the loudspeakers
signaling the show was almost over. Entranced,
I gazed at his earnest, upturned face as a sizzling
color-burst exploded behind him, dazzling, glorious.

Playbook

1

Without so much as raising a skeptical eyebrow,
      the Composition Director recounted as if reading a verdict
the lie the cunning freshman boy had just told him:

      I'd targeted him from the beginning of the term.
The truth? He'd done nothing distinctive before.
      But now I'd dared to question his polished prose,

which unspooled in a smooth argument until it snapped,
      piling into a jumbled heap of words. I was a pitiless harpy,
talons shredding the prospects of a promising young man.

      A shock wave radiated from my gut
to my brain, triggering a landslide in the terrain
      of my self-confidence. Somehow, I was the accused.

2

Only after watching decades of news clips—women
      in tailored black suits, grim-faced in courtrooms
or before Congress, their eye-witness testimony

      eviscerated by slick, smirking men—
did I realize that long-ago episode for what it was:
      a scenario from the Playbook.

3

That boy imagined me as the wrong species.
    I was a writing spider with infinite patience:
I spun my sticky signature web, then waited.

    Daily I surveilled the dim, fifth-floor library stacks
to see if a trio of books had been returned.
    Two weeks stretched tediously to three.

Then one day, the web trembled.
    With photocopied pages and a rainbow of highlighters,
I tied every plagiarized sentence to its source.

    The judiciary council hearing was open-and-shut.
I knew nothing about the Playbook, but I knew everything
    about supporting a claim with evidence.

Paradise

Newlyweds, we threw a few cassettes,
a tattered Rand McNally, and a bag of apples
into the Mazda 323—our good car—and pointed
toward the Georgia coast for our first real vacation.
Enticed by a Triple-A weekend deal in Brunswick,
we'd saved enough to splurge on a junior suite,
just one night on luxury's back doorstep.
We never imagined wandering mazy streets
where weeds were the primary householders
and instinct told us to *thunk* down our door-locks.
Baffled by wrong turns, blasted by the sour smell
of paper mills, we found the hotel at a mall
suffering the indignities of aging with the brave face
of a genteel spinster. So much for the high life.

After sunup, on to St. Simons Island, playground
of the monied classes to which we did not belong.
We spotted a motel vacancy sign in red neon
that conjured vacation scenes from childhood.
The Elysian pool was shaded by lovely old oaks
draped with Spanish moss. Who cared if the room
was small, the mattress lumpy? Paradise?
Plunging into that delicious coolness,
that delightful blue dazzle, lazily drinking in
the sky's serenity before drowsing on deck chairs
in the sun, dreaming of the better days before us.
Later we strolled down to the village to admire
the lighthouse, scrunching our toes in the sand
at low tide as shrimpers trawled along the coast.

When the phone shrilled the next morning,
our bliss shattered: Check-out in five minutes!
Threats of charges for staying a single minute over,
the manager a petty martinet flicking his whip.
Our tranquility—dawdling over rösti at a Swiss café,
swapping newspaper sections with the locals—dissolved
like the trees' reflections when we'd dived into the pool
for a last refreshing dip. Scrambling now, we clattered
up and down the stairs, the phone imperious again
as we slammed the door right on the dot. Flinging bags
into our car, we vowed, "Never again!" Next year
we would afford better. But as we sped away, I turned
for a last glimpse of light dancing on that limpid water
under those graceful, moss-draped limbs. Never again . . .

Random Act of Kindness

September 9, 2001

You scoured the Internet for a fancy restaurant
open on Sunday, looking to splurge

for our sixth anniversary: our lean years
in grad school at last yielding

a new refrigerator and washer and dryer
in our new condo, never mind

my loneliness in a new city, or the grind
of your weekly commute, 400 miles each way.

We agreed on Japanese, only to find ourselves
seated at a u-shaped *teppanyaki* table

with a dozen strangers, watching a daredevil
juggling his Ginsu knives, not our idea

of a romantic dinner for two.
Too polite to withdraw, we traded

furtive smiles and held hands under the table,
the steak and *o-sushi* rice plentiful.

A gray-haired man in a golf shirt
kept the college girls down the table laughing.

Grandfather? Or natural-born comedian?
When you slid out your wallet to pay,

the chef waved you off, nodding
toward the older man's retreating back.

"He paid for everyone. Whole table.
The world holds some good men, *ne?*"

Seizure

The guest writer sidles in, half-empty long-neck
dangling from two fingers, compact frame
listing like a clapboard shotgun shack
that's weathered too many ice storms.
His matted hair grazes his collar
like an aging rock star's. Unpromising,
we think. He barely touches his meal,
his fingers restless, fiddling with the corner
of his napkin, tracing the straight edge
of his dinner knife over and over.

Later, at the reading, we're stunned
by his mellifluous prose, dense and golden
as a jar of sun-warmed honey. Here is genius,
hidden behind the mask of a workman's face,
taut cheeks smooth as Mexican leather,
murky eyes giving away nothing. His cadences
captivate us, pulling us into the magnetic field
of his hard-scrabble imagination. We lean in,
straining to hear when his voice softens
as if a volume knob is being turned down.

Then all words stop. He hunches over the lectern,
frozen, unblinking. Is this a fit of poetic ecstasy?
When the body seizes like an engine that sputters
just before it cuts out, what happens to the soul?
Does it flutter free from its moth-frail husk
to dash itself against some unseen white-hot light?
Are we witnessing a fierce electrical storm
rumbling across a dry plain, promising relief
from its cooling breeze, or an apocalypse,
the silent implosion of a dense, bright star?

Inventory

When a woman finds a lump, she begins making lists:
clothes to drop at the dry-cleaner,
bills falling due, upcoming birthdays,
what to buy the West Coast relatives for Christmas;

> *the first-chair French horn player in district honor band*
> *the lanky basketball guard with the untamable cowlick*
> *the chemistry major who splurged on an orchid corsage*

insurance claim filing deadlines, documents to download,
prescriptions, passwords for online accounts,
access codes, the pest control schedule,
and all dental appointments for six months;

> *sweeping snow-angel wings under a star-sprinkled sky*
> *swinging out over the lake's deep dazzle on a tractor tire*
> *skimming toward Diamond Head, backlit by the city's glow*

casserole recipes easily doubled and frozen,
names of carpool drivers, babysitters' numbers,
the dates of the children's immunizations,
their t-shirt and shoe sizes and favorite desserts;

> *drenched by the scent of orange blossoms in full flower*
> *fired by the last gold light pooling on the bed*
> *soothed by the idle murmur of willows outside the window*

where Nonna's amethyst necklace is tucked away,
who gets her pearl earrings, where the will is filed,
what's on the organ donor card, and who's invited to the party
if the pathology report comes back clean.

The Train from Oxford

The railcar is insufferably hot. No one told me
there's no air conditioning because no one
owes me—a stranger—an explanation. Besides,
artificially cooled air is seldom needed here,
unlike where I come from. So I blot up
my trickles of sweat with a limp tissue
and peel shoes and socks from sore feet
chafed by unaccustomed miles of walking
amid jostling throngs of tourists chattering
a dozen languages. So much for dreaming
spires. As the train gains speed the scenery
greens and I lean back to let it flow by me,
a balm to over-stimulated senses, numb
from sorting through so much newness,
so much antiquity. Heat-hazy fields and trees
flash past, foreign, yet reminders of home.

By the time we reach Reading I've stopped
drawing comparisons. I push all thoughts
from my mind of boarding tomorrow's plane
to wrench the space-time continuum once more
and gaze at what's passing,
no longer sifting, only shedding, letting go.
Approaching Slough, I see him—
window open, arms resting along the sill,
his face beatific, like a saint's, as he watches
trains from his fourth-story pensioner's flat.
Delight in an afternoon's pastime
has erased all care-lines. For an instant,
eternity. Then he is gone, a glimpse,
a vestige, but his the face I'll remember
out of thousands, a benediction
to carry me back home.

The Moment I Realized

I would never have children
happened when she said over the phone,

". . . the way you felt when you knew
you'd never have children."

The blood rushed in my ears
like a mud-swollen torrent

tumbling over loosened boulders,
tearing at exposed tree roots,

my vision dimming as if gusts
were flapping the power lines

like limp jump-ropes,
their high-pitched whine

a keening—the sorrow
of generations of barren women

not blessed to be meddling Sarah,
or grief-drunk, importunate Hannah.

Aftermath

The silence after the storm ravages,
numbing the senses. No birds sing.
Instinct unites them in reverence
for the wreckage of limbs
where they might have been nesting,
now strewn about as carelessly
as a child's pick-up sticks.
No dogs bark. They cower under beds,
noses buried in their paws, still
cringing at the thunder's treachery,
disavowing the testimony
of a clock's soft ticking.
Only a black-and-white cat
picking its way through leafy debris
as it crosses the wet pavement
remains undeafened by the tumult's end.

Puzzle

We were a puzzling family.
I learned early to look for the straight edges first,
to form the frame, then fill in the picture.

My father seldom spoke, never of the war
unless pressed, then only tales tourists tell—
seeing Parliament, hearing Big Ben chime.

It took patience to search for the missing bits
of blue sky or red barn, shapes emerging slowly
from the hundreds of jumbled fragments.

We coaxed one story from him: a concert
in Rheims, the bemused conductor reprising the encore—
the William Tell Overture—to cheering American troops.

After supper, radio tuned to the Dodgers game,
we would work companionably, consulting the box lid
for guidance, fixing its photograph in our minds.

With only a rudimentary knowledge of history,
of school textbooks' sanitized versions of war,
I didn't know the right questions to ask.

Sometimes my mother might hover a few minutes
and pop a piece in before returning to her chores,
leaving us to the luxury of our slow, methodical work.

Over the years we progressed from orderly scenes
of rural contentment to chaotic masses of autumn foliage
and blinding white snowscapes, their shadows blue-gray,

my father living more and more in memory,
the record-player-needle of his mind skipping
and landing in unheard grooves from the past.

One day a picture of the barren French countryside
coalesced, a wintry tableau
of townspeople gathered in the square,

men shouting curses, spitting on a woman
with the shaved head of a collaborator,
the mob dragging her from the back of an army truck.

As my father talked, he began to cry,
something I'd never seen before,
and at last, all the pieces snapped into place.

Pilgrimage

At the international deli, our lunch plates a diaspora
of spanakopita and spring rolls,
Polish sausage and sweet potatoes,
Bob Marley's radio-ghost urges us to unite,
one love, one heart.
So we press past the ice-cream-vendor crush
to join the kaleidoscope of Fourth of July revelers
swirling through Battery Park—bus drivers,
nannies, piano teachers—who've proclaimed,
Today we're gathering together to celebrate!

We pause to pay homage to *The Immigrants,*
their bronze faces lifted skyward, gazing
past One World Tower as if pleading,
Have mercy on those whose hopes are dwindling!
or down on their knees, wondering,
Can a wretch find a welcome here?
or shouting with upraised hands,
We give gratitude to God!
for having survived fetid air and rancid food
on the harrowing passage to freedom.

We stroll toward the harbor to hail Lady Liberty,
who beckons with her eternal torch held high,
exhorting, *Listen to the cries of the children!*
We picture fragile limbs blasted by bombs,
imagine welcoming arms lifting tiny bodies
from half-submerged life-rafts. As our hearts sing,
From everlasting to the end of days! Amen!
we vow never to forget the sag-shouldered refugees,
the hollow-eyed veterans, the ash-grimed police
and firemen who expended their love and hearts for all.

Lipstick

My mother always wore the same shade of lipstick,
no matter what: Magnet Red, named as if color
could be an irresistible force, the ultimate come-hither.

Once as a teenager she'd suffered
a severe sunburn, her lips blistering,
a mistake she wouldn't make again.

She never went outside without protection.
During the Great Depression
she spent a hot July picking apricots

and working in the drying sheds,
a relief after trailing her father
and older sister through migrant camps,

sleeping in tents with strangers all around,
her mother and younger brothers
safe in their beds back home.

My aunt varied her lipstick palette,
radiating confidence even though her husband
turned out to be a womanizing louse,

but my mother kept everything simple, subdued, always
makeup-free except for the shade that never altered,
her only other adornment a string of drugstore beads.

That bright red seemed a beacon
when I was small, calling me to the safe harbor
of her skirts. I never asked questions

even after she warned me about men
with a story about a cad in a convertible
who'd beckoned her over and exposed himself.

Not until I was grown did I begin
to see her wound-bright mouth
as an angry slash,

a warning to steer clear,
and realize that years earlier
she'd reversed that magnet's pole.

Ghost Planes

Near midnight, through the wide kitchen window
of our darkened Memphis rental
we watch a dim light materialize in the mist,
mesmerizing us like a UFO dancing in the distance.

Its gleam separates into three white beams
intensifying with each pulse of a trailing red blink,
the monster rumbling closer, sound rippling
as if from waves crashing against a steep shingle.

With its smooth belly and angled fins, the behemoth
glides over us, deafening us with its bellow.
Behind that bulk spread-eagled against the city-glow,
a nascent light-fuzz glimmers, next in line.

One after another, the giant carriers soar past,
a scattered flock returning home to roost.
For hours we lie awake, listening to each rush
of wind, picturing wings cleaving the roiling air.

Finally, a respite. Rain drifts in, its patter
soothing, inviting deep sleep. At dawn
the great migration resumes, but invisible now,
the milky sky dense with low clouds.

Our hearts race at that unseen clamor
roaring aloft as if the heavens hold highways
for ravening beasts and archangels,
for ghostly agents of mercy and desire.

Quality of Life

Seeing my mother
curled in on herself
like a spiral shell
on a bed with a metal side-rail
was like hearing the high wail
of a far-off ambulance
late at night, its keening
faint yet persistent.

The rise and fall
of her chest barely visible,
her body's memory seemed
to beckon her back to a womb,
but that icy hospital room
was a poor replica
of the warm, dark safety
of her first home.

I spoke to her,
hoping she would wake,
but she was wandering
dream-meadows, elsewhere.
Bereft, I could only stare
at her spindle-thin legs,
her pale skin translucent
as rice paper.

I took it all in:
the stark white sheets,
the fetal curl, the fragile bones,
the shallow breath.
The shadow of death,
I realized, had begun to edge
across the late afternoon
of her remaining days.

In that moment
I grasped the meaning
of the phrase I'd often heard.
Her body might, for a time, uncurl,
but all too soon she'd furl
her bird-like limbs for good,
fold her gnarled hands, let go
a last, regretful sigh.

Condolence

The ground-scar of my father's grave has healed.
Beside it, a fresh wound: lacerated grass
marking my mother's new resting place,
rewarding her tenacity of ninety-two years.
Too raw to speak, I let the cooling air
salve me as I sit, stone-limbed, alone
but for my husband, his discreet gift
space apart and silence.

I lift my face to survey the lush lawn,
eyes snagging on a bright bobbing across the lane:
Mylar balloons in rainbow shades
dance above a mound of fresh flowers—
a smiling white My Little Pony unicorn,
a jolly yellow "Happy Birthday" sun,
a pink Hello Kitty wishing
"Get well soon!"

Notes

"Trespass" won the 2015 Rash Award in Poetry, judged by David Kirby.

"Puzzle" won the 2017 Rash Award in Poetry, judged by Bill Brown.

"Ghost Planes" won an Honorable Mention for the 2019 Rash Award in Poetry, judged by Dorianne Laux.

"Lipstick" was selected as a *Plainsongs* Award Poem for the Summer 2021 issue.

"Random Act of Kindness" was a finalist in the 2023 Derek Burleson Poetry Contest and was selected for *The Best of Choeofpleirn Press,* Winter 2023.

"Seizure" was written in memory of novelist William Gay.

For those who may be unfamiliar with formal poetry, "Monkey Bars" is a villanelle, "Help Me" is a ghazal, and "Counterpoint" and "Paternalism" are pantoums.

Thanks to Christine Bailey, Angela D. Lee, and Lori Ann Cook-Neisler for their technical assistance.

About the Author

Southern California native Patricia L. Hamilton earned her Ph.D. at the University of Georgia. Newly retired as a professor of English, she served in higher education for forty years. She won the 2015 and 2017 Rash Award in Poetry and has received three Pushcart Prize nominations.

Her poetry has been published in *Broad River Review, Ibbetson Street, Innisfree Poetry Journal,* and *Plainsongs,* among other journals. She resides in Jackson, Tennessee, with her husband and enjoys travel, jazz, mystery novels, and a good cappuccino.

www.ingramcontent.com/pod-product-compliance
Lightning Source LLC
Chambersburg PA
CBHW071011160426
43193CB00012B/2013